# *Adam's Philosophy*

DEREK JAMES

WestBow Press books may be ordered through booksellers or by contacting:

WestBow Press
A Division of Thomas Nelson & Zondervan
1663 Liberty Drive
Bloomington, IN 47403
www.westbowpress.com
1 (866) 928-1240



ISBN: 978-1-5127-8582-1 (sc)
ISBN: 978-1-5127-8583-8 (e)

Print information available on the last page.

WestBow Press rev. date: 05/12/2017

To the best of us

## Contents

*Synopsis*

Tortured Philosophy ........ 3

*Act One*

Angel Smile's Gift (1) ........ 7
Sophia's Whispers ........ 9
A Portrait of Lovers (1) ........ 11
Heaven's Tears ........ 13

*Act Two*

Angel Smile's Gift (2) ........ 17
When Sophia Smiles ........ 19
Captain of the Army ........ 21
Old Wineskins ........ 23
A Portrait of Lovers (2) ........ 25

*Act Three*

Angel Smile's Gift (3) ........ 29
Envoy at the Heathen's Table ........ 31
Posterity of Cain ........ 35
Temple Rays and the Scarlet Woman ........ 37
Angel Smile's Gift (4) ........ 39

# SYNOPSIS

## Tortured Philosophy

Dismembering into varying pieces
A puzzling and unique thesis:
On the machining of an abstract tortured genius.

An art of crafting definable
By both the simplicity of a bubble
And the complexity in the origin of a pearl –

The perfect balance of hope and struggle
To trigger an irritable reaction
To society's woes…

Forcing an outburst of expression
Willfully carving and re-shaping philosophy.

# ACT ONE

## Angel Smile's Gift (I)

Loneliness sits in the heart of the city
Earnestly searching to be lifted,
Seeking the Angel Smile's gift of kisses
To heal hearts yearning for commitment
Where Adam stands
With the world an opponent,
Lacking the element
To complete the perfect chemistry –
Early sunrise with rays of beauty.

Wake up, morning! Beauty in mind –
Her sweet scent is one of a kind
And a treatment for those scarred,
Obsessed and insane… the way we are.
Who's to blame when falling hard,
Calling love in vain and can't see that far?
Deceived in youth – chasing false stars…

Each night haunted by dreams –
Desire, a fire engulfing every tree.
Running a fever in the forest of love,
Seeing beauty in self as the only cure –
Smart to charm, crude with vanity in arms,
Cute with pride that smiles ten feet tall.
Yes, beauty classifies for all service calls.

In the heart of the city, behind city walls,
Hours conversing, kissing and caressing.
Secret rendezvous,
Entertained by lust singing sweetest taboo,
Lost in senseless sensation proves good
As enslaved in the motion of restless music –
Endless expressions of emotions made basic.

Beauty stands in mind overlooking the city...
A perfect view of the clock of reason.
Change in time – seconds to infinity...
Change in eternity's garden with season...
Once roses of hope, now thorns of weeds –
Broken plants will hardly, if ever, grow leaves
Unless nourished with the Angel Seed...

In the form of the Angel Smile's gift of kisses.
The heart of the city in its find:
Beauty – full of riches –
Becomes flawed in violence's grasp...
Squeezing out life with claws digging deep –
Joys experienced in a distant past
Like cubs in the wild born to be free...
Now grown to be hunted by mankind's cast.

## Sophia's Whispers

The silence of night
Delivers echoes of her voice
Wrapped in a gentle breeze.

Sophia's waters pierce my soul
And make me weep.
Strumming the chords of my sentiments…
And producing a melody
That mirrors the emotion with which she sings…

About the neglect she endures
In the silence of Adam's heart…
Where she sits and stares
Into the emptiness of a space
As dark and bare as the first time.

## A Portrait of Lovers (I)

Once in a while
Captivating artistry – a beautiful smile –
Perched on a table with drinks.
Sometime, maybe one time,
An extra mile in exploring psyche.

New scene, enters stupefied –
Adam, caught in a feeling divine,
Can't pass by a breath of fresh air
After a lifetime of no oxygen
Under the stench of wantonness.

Adventure begins with the thrill
Of a mission requiring intricate lessons
On patience and tolerance
To discern Sophia's intimations…
And covertly intimidate
Other persons in chance of this romance…

That starts inclined, then entwined.
These fascinating beings draw
From within, and around comes
The inner child telling everything…
As the corners of character
Pursue approval.

Voices become soothing as choice wine
From father's own vines.
Soft skin beneath fingertips
Animate unknown sensations with every sip…
Of a touch for long missed.
Every embrace of lips

Composing a sweet sound.
A band of two keeps true
To instruments playing in tune…
Singing a sweet rhythm –
A melody that stirs passion…

Into a drunken fit
Of dancing hearts pulsing with music…
As together paint, for a private display,
Portraits of frequencies,
Wavelengths and vibration…
In a realm of pleasure and affection.

## Heaven's Tears

Torrential rain – weeping for the fields –
Pours from the skies.
Aroused by heaven's tears,
The sea raises his tides –
Enraged – for his sister, washing her injuries…
Kissing cavernous scars of past centuries –
The blood spilt from wars in disaccord
With the guardians of habitations
Weakened by Adam's stab and bore
In search for oil, diamonds, gold, and ore.
Defeated, she crumbled to the shore.

Comforted by her brother,
Her might is restored.
Seeing her reflection,
She trembles in her core –
The squalor of her scenery
Instigates her fury –
Turning and churning the fire in her belly.
She opens her mouth and spews out flames –
Her cry for justice lamenting her pains.
Carried by heralds of her husband –
The wind and the black arid clouds –
A message is sent through all of Adam's lands,

"Abominable child standing proud,
As an infant I nursed you in my hands.
Today you drain my soul under the shroud
Of applying my teachings to advance.
Degrading my worth in your arrogance.
You fell the pillars that held my hair –
Full, rich and luscious – serenading the air.
My essence you drank, exploring my pit
Only to spit destructive fumes and hazardous liquids
In my husband's eyes and my brother's body.

Judgement rides vehemently
On chariots of hurricane
Rummaging cities in retribution
For your atrocities!
See the hearts of ice caps melt in trepidation!
But the crown princess Sophia may offer placation…
If you become her prince
Adorning your heart with tenderness and virtue…
Judgement will desist."

# ACT TWO

## Angel Smile's Gift (2)

Indignation infests the heart of the city,
Awakened by a branch of perjury
Trying to topple the gift of justice –
The dew at dawn from a rising mist –
Where Adam tills the soil; sowing serenity
To reap a nature that's godly,
Wise, strong, kind and lovely.

Wake up, morning! The vineyard is overrun
With locusts the size of men
And heads like that of the dragon.
They crushed our grapes –
Ravished and degraded our women,
Killed our sons and our future,
Invaded our minds and tainted our culture.

Each night haunted by dreams –
Desire, a fire engulfing every tree,
Crying for vengeance on our enemies
That took our strong as captives,
Left our land barren,
Deprived us of our children
And left the elderly empty within.

In the heart of the city lies pestilence.
Vileness has taken residence
On the seat of the prude,
Proliferating a temperament –
That of the crude –
Polluting nature's quintessence
And eating at innocence's roots.

Vengeance rides through
On the wings of the wind.
On hearing the cries of the people,
Restoration begins
Planting that which is unseen
In the core of the new offspring,
Renewing the earth with the Angel Seed.

In the form of the Angel Smile's gift of justice,
A child in the house of the vile
Draws a plan for armistice:
Summoning ones in exile
To join the just of takers in easing grudge.
For blessed are the peacemakers
That will be called sons of God.

## When Sophia Smiles

Drawn by the simplicity of her smile
And its radiance – blinding in intensity…
Every time she shines, Adam falls in love helplessly.

Entangled in the notion of an abstract word
Which in itself has no meaning –
Bound in the motion of thoughts
Instilled in the child of his upbringing.
He was raised in a stance dictated by possessions,
So in his eyes to love comes second to the object of his affection.
Hence, Sophia makes him crazed – putting him in a trance
Created by an obsession with the smile
That beckons the realization of perfection.

Trapped in a maze of confusion,
A force, built from that which dreams are made,
Takes his heart to a throne from whence it is seen
The maze is the only path home.
Through the gates of the castle he did proceed
And in the courts he was left to roam
That he may truly perceive:
Nothing belonged to him
But all is the possession of the force within.
And in that moment he was taken to the quarters bestowed on him.
Then and only then did he see…

The love of possessions is false.
For to possess love is to be possessed by love,
And in this embrace of force and being
Lays the essence of this castle of dreams.

So you see, all along it was his love that called to him
With the simplicity of a smile…
And, having a radiance blinding in intensity,
Every time Sophia shines he falls in love helplessly.

## Captain of the Army

Stimulating in her approach to everything she encounters
Like an athlete meeting a coach –
A descendant of co-founders –
Of the sport she's determined to dominate.

In her rite, Sophia is a master of games.
In psyche, profusely training and pushing weights,
Her mind like the engines of an aeroplane:
Non-reciprocating from the moment of ignition.

Yesterday's errs, today's fuel for combustion.
In the day's first conscious breath,
She exhales yesterday's exhaustive delusions.

Taking on each day furnished in her amour –
An array of garments complementing her frame.
A master architect's work designed with opaque windows
Veiling that of which she's made.

Empathic and crafty in her business,
Graceful as a dove…
Yet, with a bite that doesn't fail
To sting and torment contenders of her seal.

Mystery and wonder lay behind those eyes.
Mesmerized, Adam signed on the dotted line.
Giving her authority to carry his name
And bear his children… but not in vain.

## Old Wineskins

New wine in old
Wineskins –
The feeling this sensual fruit brings:
Invigorating and elating to hold;
Full of much life
Threatening to explode,
From the seams,
A vessel
Worn fetching dreams.

New love in a new day –
A new age of gold.
"Exercise restraint and caution,
Lest it unfold
Into crisis." Whispers
The distant voice of reason
Lurking in the shadow.

New wine in old
Wineskins –
The feeling this lustful drink gives:
Exhilarating and animating to hold;
Full of much life
Bubbling to overflow,
Sealing and cascading
A vessel
In an initial youthful glow.

New love in a new day –
A new age of gold…
Days pass
And ages grow old…
Or are cut short –
Poisoned by forbidden fruit damning the soul,
Yet sweet to taste and touch.

## A Portrait of Lovers (2)

The captivating artistry
In the fusion of sexes.
Two becoming both home and gallery,
Soul and body, and one frame of memories…
Lakes endowed with springs

Fed through hidden streams
From divine oceans... a scenery
Complete in its entirety…
Valleys and rocky mountains…
Captured in an eternal glimpse…

Displaying an adventurous journey
Of devotion morphing to assurance…
With patience and tolerance
Teaching co-habitation
And eliminating every doubt
Or need for external insurance.

Never untwined, these two of a kind…
Of fascinating being.
Recreating self in birth –
Images varying slightly
In the corners of character…
Yet, similar…

Voices forever soothing as choice wine
From lover's own vines.
More so when grey with little to enjoy…
Made merry with every sip…
Of joy and laughter from merits –
Sons, daughters and grandkids…

Compose sweet a sound.
All in band keep true
To instruments playing in tune –
Singing a sweet rhythm.
A melody of weekend and holiday visits
Lost in broken chords from a missing string…

When arrives the moment of a half's departure…
Travelling a path… a realm unseen
To the bereaved that considers it fantasy,
As with Adam, and hence retreats…
Hiding exhibitions of portraits
In a section titled, SOPHIA: ALL MEET FATE.

# ACT THREE

## Angel Smile's Gift (3)

Frustration attacks the heart of the city
With the intention to annihilate sanity
And imprison the gift of peace;
Keeping a fortified city under siege
Where Adam works with forest beasts
Producing grains in vast variety –
Some for gain, some to feed the country.

Wake up, morning! Terror sounds the alarm.
Animals are restless and fear fills the streets.
The city has no sense of calm.
Mothers and children scurry to flee
A town left desolate and
A great prince brought to his knees –
Caged by that which he craves...

Each night haunted by dreams –
Desire, a fire engulfing every tree,
Yearning to be glorified above all.
Egocentric adulation – the why we fall.
Diabolic exhortation as the tutor
And treachery's begetter, the author
Of destruction, masquerading as the narrator.

In the heart of the city, the false prophet
Disguised as an angel of light
Secretly prepares the city's plummet;
Blinding understanding with the cloak of night,
Commanding the people to sacrifice.
Husbands in their delusion swallow their wives –
Dishonoring a holy union and the bed that's undefiled.

Glory sits in his room, troubled by distress.
In a moment of clarity,
In comes the realization of self.
Once free in safety and undisturbed by death,
Now burdened with worry
And the threat of ill-health.
The remedy found only in the Angel Seed.

In the form of the Angel Smile's gift of peace,
A true prince sees
Discontentment opens the doors to misery...
Allowing false doctrines
Concealed as mysteries
To hold all it can
In the hands of perversity.

## Envoy at the Heathen's Table

Incognito, an envoy walks the streets
Observing the brethren
Endeavour to make ends meet.

A part openly breaks capitalists'
Prescribed laws – heathen –
Others are more discreet.
Most are victims to proscribed customs
Subconsciously daunting the discrete.

The envoy finds amusement
In the heathen's outright rebellion –
Questioning the scribes of heaven –
And quest for freedom.

Discreet lawbreakers dance
In ritualistic celebrations
Commemorating the falsehood
Of law makers;
Masquerades on display,
Sirens announce approach,
Costumes to astonish
And whips for the citizens
Of reproach and admonish –
The honest of the breed,
Despised of the bunch,
Hearts on sleeves

Rolling with the punch,
Loyal to self and own, heathen,
Professing inconformity
Of mind, body and soul
To dictatorship – a usurping capitalist's system.

Incognito, the envoy walks the streets
Observing his brethren
Endeavour to make ends meet.

The part openly breaks capitalists'
Prescribed laws – heathen –
The others are more discreet.
Most are victims of proscribed customs
Subconsciously wanting to be discrete.
The many embrace the mark of the beast,
Resisting being separate
And yet, trying to be distinct.

Discreet lawbreakers
Dance in ritualistic celebrations
Commemorating the falsehood
Of law makers –
Masquerades in the show,
Sirens announce approach,
Costumes to daze

And speakerphones to orate
Ire for the zealot's inability
To commend hypocrisy
And share in the mend of ill-normality.

"Crucify him, crucify him,
The envoy welcome at the heathen's table!"
Hallucinating behind masks –
Adam, now a dissident incognito.

## Posterity of Cain

Jezebel!
You that clothe yourself in the finest of fabrics
And adorn yourself in expensive jewellery!
You paint your many faces
And put your hair in braids
Trying to disguise your ugliness
And hide your shame.

Daughter of deceit!
Friend amongst friends...
You that stir animosity
By giving into the lusts of your flesh!

Offspring of the adulteress and sorceress!
You that pounce, and hound
Men in their sleep!
You say, "Men are dogs!"
You lay with them and conceive wild beasts...

Consumed by envy, despair, and hate.
Jezebel! Depart from the destructive ways
Of your father – Cain!

## Temple Rays and the Scarlet Woman

The sun's risen and walks across the sky,
Shining in its radiance…
Beautiful and perfect to the good eye,
Saying, "You that desires to see,
Come and receive eyes that shine bright
That you may always have light."

In this generation, the scarlet woman
Roams the streets at night,
Seeking a means to satisfy a longing for life,
But, in confusion, always fails to listen
To the many calls of the light of day.

In the rays of sun, peace calls to her saying,
"A new day comes! The king of all the land calls you
To stay awake at his temple and wait on his return,
That you may join in his banquet
And sit amongst kings and great princes."

The scarlet woman enjoys the street life.
Blinded by desires for fortune and fame,
Drunk from the adulterous wine that steals life,
She staggers in the rain, holding over her head
An umbrella of worthless gain.

Horizon says, "To the good eye that shines bright,
Stay awake, all is well for you are at the temple gates.
But for you who love the night
And roam the dark streets, seek the light
That you may find the way to the king's feast."

Intoxicated by vanity's fumes,
The scarlet woman says,
"There is still time before daybreak.
I will satisfy myself in the streets before dawn
And catch a night bus to the temple gates.
After all, the king's men are kind
And I am a thing of beauty."

Twilight comes with a message in a gentle wind,
"In preparation for his return,
The king sends forth
Chariots of tornado and hurricane
To cleanse the land with quakes and flames.
Woe to you, O Jezebel, outside his temple gates!"

## Angel Smile's Gift (4)

Enervation preys on the heart of the city,
Awaiting the appropriate opportunity –
The absence of the gift of strength –
To spread its pinions and devour wealth and authority
Where Cain leads his family brazenly,
Yet with some modesty,
Blind to the lurking animosity.

Wake up, morning! All vigor is gone –
Extinguished in the rigor of wanting more.
Distinguished eyesores, claiming wisdom,
Relinquish habitation to kidnap freedom.
Anguish is reality, yet trapped in illusion –
Law enforcement for security,
Raw surveillance to map detention.

Each night haunted by dreams –
Desire, a fire engulfing every tree…
A troubled mind is what it seems,
Says books on psychology.
Anything else, how can it be? All's taught in education –
Life, history, the birds and the bees…
Syllabus of worthlessness passed through generations.

In the heart of the city dwells confusion,
Born to weakness
And raised by dispossession
In the house of foolishness;
The spouse of ignorance
Filled with eagerness for a glance
Of self in broken glass.

Knowledge breaks through
On the stem of truth,
Brought forth in an ancient book –
Scripts of priests
Preserved through time
As a gift of words –
The Angel Seed. In it a sword

In the form of the Angel Smile's gift of strength.
Cain turns to Adam's quest for beauty
To re-establish a kingdom
Providing rest and shelter
In this here desert storm…
Where lives pain and turmoil so great…
And silent hopes for Sophia's waters to liberate…